HIDDEN MAGIC!

Cover design: Stabenfeldt AS

ISBN: 978-1-934983-36-2
Editor: Bobbie Chase

Printed in Denmark

Stabenfeldt, Inc.
225 Park Avenue South
New York, NY 10003
www.pony4kids.com

Available exclusively through PONY.

Meet **Mandy Ferris.** She's a stable hand at **SuperRide** – the fastest, flashiest amusement park in town.

SuperRide was once owned by her **grandfather,** but was bought by the mean **Mister Mockley** (whose daughter, **Penelope**, is a REAL pain)!

When she's not grooming the park horses with her friend **Dino**, Mandy and her father, **Mike**, restore their pride and joy – an old carousel from days gone by. But amidst the ghost trains and roller coasters, Mandy uncovers a secret that makes the carousel the greatest ride of them all!

With the help of **Madame Zingara** and the **triplets** (Ting, Zing and Ling) can Mandy and her new best friend stop Mr. Mockley from selling the carousel AND keep their incredible secret from a world that will tear them apart?

Mandy Ferris
Mandy's special friendship with horses makes her a great stable hand... and the perfect person to guard the Carousel's big secret!

Midnight
Midnight is an unusual Carousel horse... so unusual, in fact, that he comes alive when Mandy needs his help!

Penelope Mockley
Heir-apparent to the Mockley fortune, Penelope is suspicious of Mandy, and determined to uncover her secret!
Mr. Mockley
Mr. Mockley only likes rides that turn a big profit, which means the Carousel is always at the top of his hit-list.
Dino
Dino is Mandy's best human friend. He's always there with a smile… a smile that Mandy really likes!
Zing, Ling & Ting
The world's greatest sideshow must be the balancing act of Chinese triplets Zing, Ling and Ting. Don't try this at home!!
Madame Zingara
Mysterious, magical and motherly… Madame Zingara is Mandy's connection to the past, and the Carousel's great history!
Mike Ferris
Mike's life mission is to protect the Carousel, which reminds him of his father and wife, from the conniving Mr. Mockley!

MANDY IS SPENDING SOME TIME WITH HER SPECIAL FRIEND BEFORE THE CONSTRUCTION WORKERS ARRIVE TO COMPLETE THE SUPERRIDE RENOVATIONS.
OH, MIDNIGHT, I CAN'T WAIT FOR YOU TO MEET THE NEW HORSE. SHE'S SO BEAUTIFUL. IN FACT SHE USED TO BE A SHOW HORSE.
MR. MOCKLEY THINKS PENELOPE STANDS A BETTER CHANCE OF WINNING IF SHE TRAINS WITH HER.
I THINK PENELOPE WOULD STAND A BETTER CHANCE OF WINNING IF SHE DIDN'T TREAT HER HORSES SO BADLY.
WHO COULD BE COMING HERE SO EARLY?

YOU'D BETTER DISAPPEAR, MIDNIGHT.

DADDY, LOOK. THE PAPARAZZI ARE HERE TO TAKE PHOTOS OF MY PRIZE-WINNING SHOW HORSE.
MAKE SURE YOU GET A SHOT OF THE HORSES IN THE STABLES.
WE'RE WITH ANIMAL NEWS NETWORK, INVESTIGATING ALLEGATIONS OF MISTREATMENT OF THESE RESCUE HORSES.
MISTREAT. . . THAT'S ABSURD!
SO YOU WON'T MIND IF WE HAVE A LOOK AT YOUR LATEST ADDITION?
THIS HORSE WAS A GIFT FROM THE HEWITTS . . . YOU KNOW, THE ANNUAL HEWITT HORSE SHOW!
THAT'S RIGHT. FINE SPECIMEN, ISN'T SHE?
THWAP
NEEEEIIGHH
GET OUT OF THE WAY, PENELOPE!

PLEASE CALM DOWN. IT'S ALRIGHT, WE'RE ALL FRIENDS HERE.

GOOD GIRL.
LET'S GET HER INSIDE.

THAT'S AMAZING. I THINK SHE'S REALLY LISTENING TO ME.

SHE SEEMS VERY ANXIOUS, MOCKLEY. I WONDER HOW MR. HEWITT WOULD FEEL IF HE KNEW HIS PRIZED SHOW HORSE WAS BEING SO MISTREATED.

I ASSURE YOU THAT THIS HORSE WILL BE GIVEN THE BEST POSSIBLE CARE.

WE'LL BE BACK IN TWO DAYS TO MAKE SURE YOU KEEP YOUR PROMISE, MOCKLEY.
OKAY, CREW. THAT'S A WRAP.

IF THIS HORSE DOESN'T CALM DOWN, DINO, IT'LL BE ON YOUR HEAD.
MR. MOCKLEY, MANDY AND I ARE DOING THE BEST WE CAN. MAYBE IF THE HORSES HAD A LITTLE MORE SPACE . . .
THE HORSES JUST NEED PROPER TREATMENT, MR. MOCKLEY. YOU CAN'T BE TOO ROUGH WITH THEM.
THE STABLES ARE FINE! AND I CAN TREAT THE HORSES HOWEVER I WANT. THESE ARE MY HORSES.
WHY DON'T YOU TRY CALMING IT THEN, MANDY? UNLESS YOU'RE JUST ALL TALK!
ME?!
WHY NOT YOU? YOU ALWAYS GO ON AND ON ABOUT PROPER GROOMING AND NOT MISTREATING THE HORSES, BLAH BLAH BLAH . . .
A PERSON WHO DIDN'T KNOW ANY BETTER MIGHT ASSUME YOU HAVE A HORSE OF YOUR VERY OWN.

I'VE ALWAYS WANTED TO SEE IF I CAN COMMUNICATE WITH OTHER HORSES THE WAY I DO WITH MIDNIGHT.

COME ON, MANDY. JUST IGNORE PENELOPE.
PLEASE DON'T TRAMPLE ME . . .

HI. I'M MANDY, A FRIEND. YOU'RE SAFE HERE.

NEEEEIIGHH
OH, NO!
HA HA! MANDY, THAT LOOK OF FEAR ON YOUR FACE IS PRICELESS.
THE HORSE SIMPLY DOESN'T WANT ANYONE NEAR IT.
YOU HAVE TWO DAYS TO GET THAT ANIMAL UNDER CONTROL!

DON'T FEEL BAD, MANDY. AT LEAST YOU TRIED.
I HAD HER UNDER CONTROL. SHE SPOOKED WHEN PENELOPE SHONE THAT LIGHT IN HER EYES.

HOW DO YOU KNOW?
SHE TOLD ME.
WAIT! AM I . . . ACTUALLY UNDERSTANDING HORSES NOW?

UM . . . IT DOESN'T MATTER. LET'S NAME HER. THE MOCKLEYS MAY NOT CARE, BUT SHE CAN'T BE "THE NEW HORSE" FOREVER.

GOOD POINT. WHAT ABOUT SOMETHING LIKE APRIL . . . OR MAY?
MAYBE IF SHE WAS A LITTLE PONY. A STRONG HORSE NEEDS A STRONG NAME.

UM, WELL . . . THOSE ARE MY SUGGESTIONS. WHAT'RE YOURS?
LOOK HOW HER COAT CATCHES THE SUNLIGHT. LIKE A SUNRISE.

SUNRISE! ONCE SHE'S GROOMED, SHE'LL GLOW LIKE A SUNRISE.
SUNRISE. I LIKE IT. I'D BETTER GET GOING. I PROMISED THE CONSTRUCTION WORKERS I'D LEND THEM A HAND.

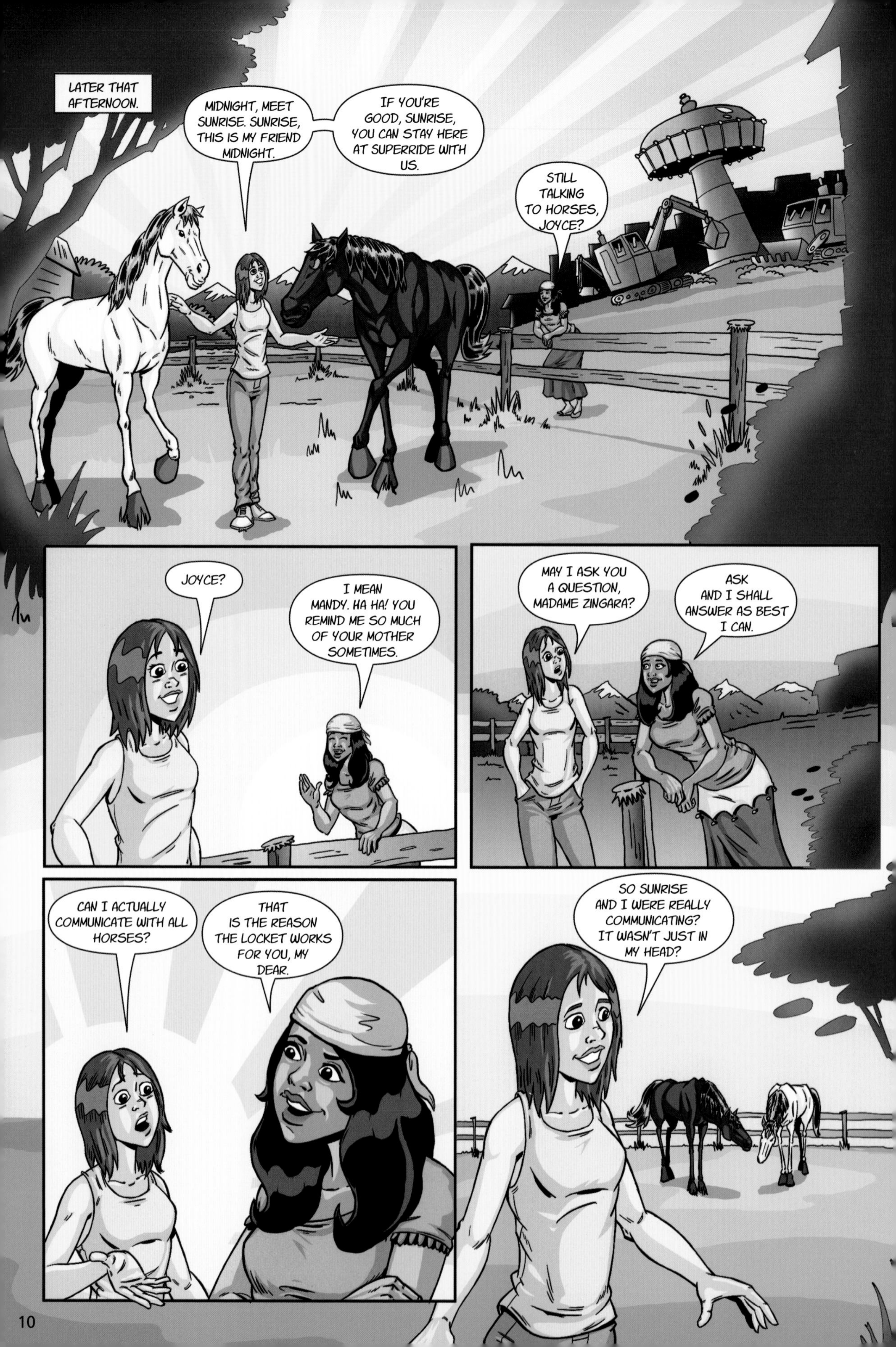
LATER THAT AFTERNOON.
MIDNIGHT, MEET SUNRISE. SUNRISE, THIS IS MY FRIEND MIDNIGHT.
IF YOU'RE GOOD, SUNRISE, YOU CAN STAY HERE AT SUPERRIDE WITH US.
STILL TALKING TO HORSES, JOYCE?
JOYCE?
I MEAN MANDY. HA HA! YOU REMIND ME SO MUCH OF YOUR MOTHER SOMETIMES.
MAY I ASK YOU A QUESTION, MADAME ZINGARA?
ASK AND I SHALL ANSWER AS BEST I CAN.
CAN I ACTUALLY COMMUNICATE WITH ALL HORSES?
THAT IS THE REASON THE LOCKET WORKS FOR YOU, MY DEAR.
SO SUNRISE AND I WERE REALLY COMMUNICATING? IT WASN'T JUST IN MY HEAD?

THE LOCKET ONLY WORKS FOR PEOPLE WHO HAVE THE ABILITY TO COMMUNICATE WITH HORSES AND HAVE A GREATER UNDERSTANDING OF HOW NATURE IS LINKED TO MAGIC.
BUT I DON'T KNOW ANYTHING ABOUT MAGIC, EXCEPT THAT IT EXISTS.

THERE IS MORE MAGIC IN YOU THAN YOU REALIZE. ALL THAT IS REQUIRED OF YOU IS TO FIND IT.

I GUESS IT'S TIME I TOLD YOU ABOUT YOUR MOTHER AND THE CONNECTION YOU BOTH HAVE TO THE LOCKET.

YES, PLEASE. HOW WELL DID YOU KNOW MY MOTHER?
YOUR MOTHER AND I MET WHEN WE WERE EVEN YOUNGER THAN YOU ARE NOW, MANDY.

YOUR MOTHER HAD JUST MOVED TO TOWN WHEN SHE CAME TO THE PARK. THE PLACE WAS FALLING DOWN, BUT THE CAROUSEL STILL WORKED.
HI, I'M MIRELA.
I'M JOYCE. NICE TO MEET YOU.
YOUR MOTHER LOVED HORSES BUT THERE WAS NO MONEY FOR STABLES THEN, SO YOUR MOTHER AND I USED TO RIDE THE CAROUSEL AND PRETEND.
I THINK I'LL HAVE TO CALL MY HORSE MIDNIGHT.
ONE DAY WE CAME ACROSS THE LOCKET IN MY MOTHER'S CHEST. I URGED JOYCE TO PUT IT ON BECAUSE IT WENT SO NICELY WITH HER OUTFIT.
OH IT'S BEAUTIFUL!

WE USED THE CAROUSEL IN PRETEND GAMES, TO TRANSPORT TO MAGICAL WORLDS.
WE MUST BE NEARING THE CASTLE BY NOW.
AND ONCE WE'RE THERE YOU CAN PROVE THAT YOU ARE THE MOST POWERFUL FORTUNE TELLER IN ALL THE LAND, MIRELA!

THAT DAY SOMETHING SURPRISING HAPPENED.
HURRY UP, MIDNIGHT. WE HAVE TO REACH THE CASTLE!

MIDNIGHT IS THE SAME HORSE?! I THOUGHT THE ORIGINAL HORSE WAS LOST WHEN MY GRANDFATHER SOLD IT!
HOW MANY MAGICAL CAROUSEL HORSES DO YOU THINK THERE ARE? AND HOW MANY DO YOU THINK THIS LOCKET WILL BRING TO LIFE?
I DON'T KNOW. I GUESS IT NEVER OCCURRED TO ME.
I ALWAYS KNEW WHERE MIDNIGHT WAS AND, WHEN THE TIME CAME, SIMPLY POINTED YOUR DAD IN THE RIGHT DIRECTION.
DOES MY DAD KNOW ABOUT ANY OF THIS?
THAT YOU WILL HAVE TO FIND OUT FOR YOURSELF.
I THINK YOU SHOULD HAVE THIS.
IT WAS TAKEN JUST BEFORE MIDNIGHT WAS SOLD.
RUMBLE RUMBLE
RUMBLE RUMBLE
I'LL TAKE SUNRISE INSIDE. SHE DOESN'T LIKE THE CONSTRUCTION NOISE.

EARLY THE NEXT MORNING . . .
RUMBLE! RUMBLE!
ZZ
ZZ
ZZ
WHAT'S THAT NOISE?
OH, IT MUST BE THE CONSTRUCTION WORKERS STARTING ON THE ROLLER COASTER.
THANK GOODNESS, I CAN GO BACK TO SLEEP.
BZZZZ
SUNRISE? OH, NO!

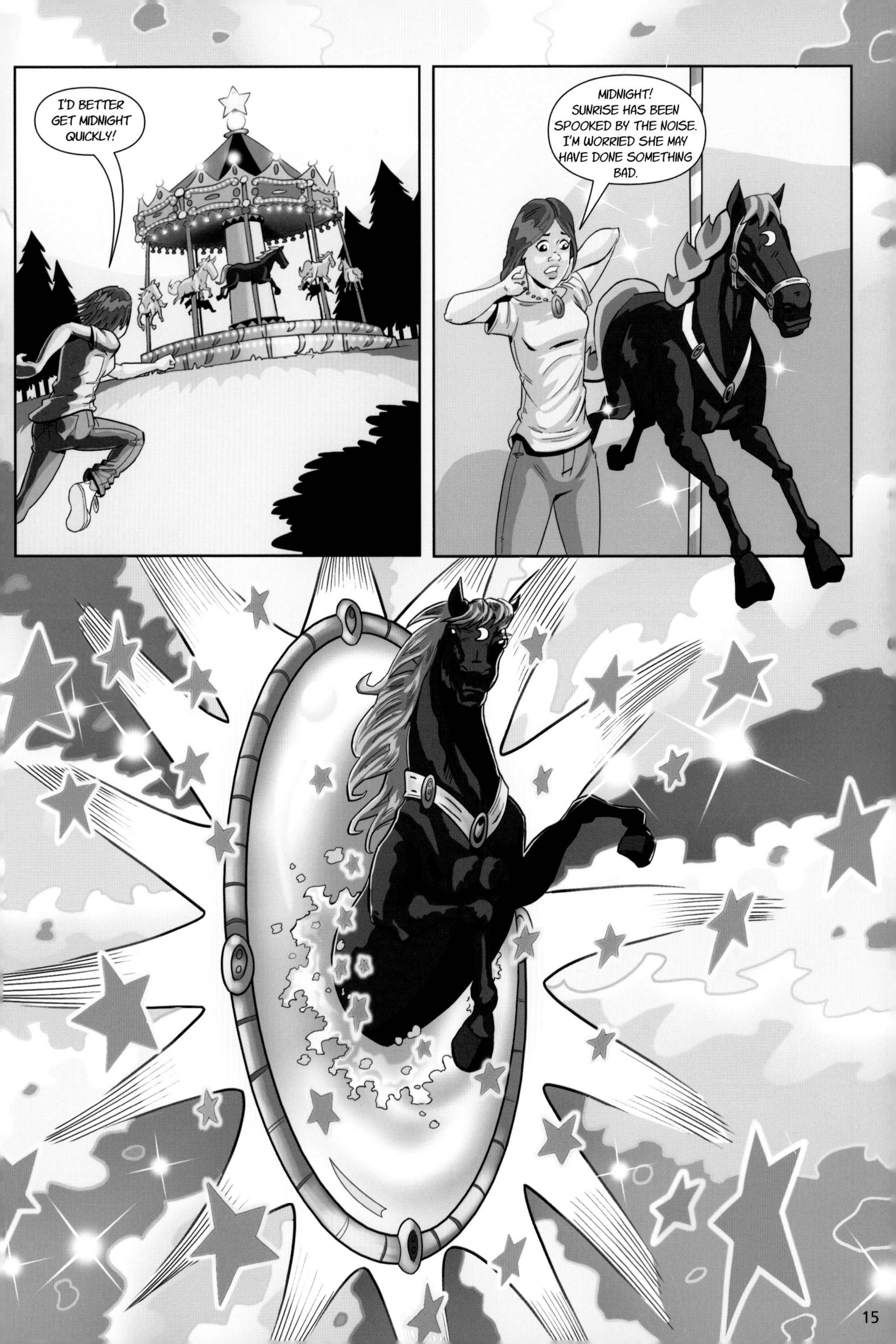
I'D BETTER GET MIDNIGHT QUICKLY!
MIDNIGHT! SUNRISE HAS BEEN SPOOKED BY THE NOISE. I'M WORRIED SHE MAY HAVE DONE SOMETHING BAD.

WE'RE TOO LATE! THE HORSES HAVE ALL BOLTED THROUGH THE HOLE SUNRISE MADE!
PHEW! THERE THEY ARE. BUT WHERE'S SUNRISE?
WHAT SHOULD WE DO, MIDNIGHT? WE CAN'T LEAVE THEM OUT HERE ON THEIR OWN. BUT MR. MOCKLEY WILL KILL ME IF WE CAN'T FIND SUNRISE.
THANK YOU, MIDNIGHT. WHILE YOU GO AFTER SUNRISE, I'LL TAKE THE OTHERS BACK TO THE STABLES.
MADAME ZINGARA WAS RIGHT. I REALLY CAN COMMUNICATE WITH HORSES.
COME ON, BOBO.

DADDY! DADDY, COME QUICKLY! MANDY LET THAT NEW HORSE BREAK THE FENCE. NOW ALL THE HORSES ARE LOOSE!
WHAT?! SHE WAS SUPPOSED TO BE CALMING THE HORSE!

MANDY, WHAT'S GOING ON?
SUNRISE ACCIDENTALLY KNOCKED DOWN THE FENCE.

THIS IS GOING TO TAKE SOME FIXING.
AND MOCKLEY'S NOT GOING TO BE TOO HAPPY, EITHER.
I'M JUST WORRIED ABOUT SUNRISE. I HOPE THAT MID-

YOU HOPE WHAT, MANDY?
I HOPE I CAN FIND HER.
YES, MANDY, YOU HAD BETTER FIND THAT HORSE!

THE REPORTERS FROM ANIMAL NEWS NETWORK ARE ON THEIR WAY, AND IF THEY FIND OUT YOU LET THIS HAPPEN THEY'LL TAKE ALL THE HORSES AWAY.

I WON'T LET THAT HAPPEN. I'M GOING TO GET SUNRISE.
I'LL GO WITH YOU.
OH NO! YOU AND MIKE ARE STAYING RIGHT HERE UNTIL THIS FENCE IS FIXED!

GRR . . . RUINED MY DAY! THAT HORSE IS RUINING MY LIFE!
IT'S ALL RIGHT. I'LL BE FINE.

I DON'T THINK IT'S SUCH A GOOD IDEA, LETTING HER GO AFTER A SCARED HORSE ON HER OWN.
MANDY WILL BE FINE. SHE HAS A WAY WITH HORSES. JUST LIKE HER MOTHER.

MIDNIGHT FOUND SUNRISE. THANK GOODNESS.
THEY'RE SO HAPPY TOGETHER.
NEEEEIGGGGHH
IT'S JUST ME, SUNRISE. IT'S MANDY.
I KNOW YOU'RE SCARED, SUNRISE. BUT WE NEED TO GO BACK TO THE STABLE NOW . . .
. . . SO THE REPORTERS CAN SEE THAT YOU WANT TO STAY HERE.
DON'T WORRY, SUNRISE. MIDNIGHT AND I WON'T LET ANYTHING HAPPEN TO YOU.

THEY'RE HERE ALREADY?
WE'RE HERE TO CHECK UP ON THE SHOW HORSE, MOCKLEY. AND IF ANYTHING SEEMS BELOW STANDARD, WE'LL TAKE HER BACK WITH US.
SEE FOR YOURSELF. SHE'S THERE . . . SOMEWHERE.
DADDY, THIS HORSE IS TOO MUCH FUSS. LET'S JUST GET RID OF IT.
PENNYKINS, IF HEWITT FINDS OUT WE'VE LOST HIS SHOW HORSE OUR REPUTATION IN THE EQUESTRIAN CIRCLE WILL BE RUINED.
YOU'D BETTER HIDE, MIDNIGHT.

WHAT ARE YOU TRYING TO PULL, MOCKLEY? THE PRIZED SHOW HORSE ISN'T HERE.

THAT'S BECAUSE SHE'S RIGHT HERE.
WHERE DID YOU FIND THE HORSE, YOUNG LADY? HOW DID YOU MANAGE TO CALM HER DOWN?

NNEEEIIIGGHH
EASY, SUNRISE! IT'S OKAY.
YOUNG LADY, DO YOU HONESTLY BELIEVE THAT HORSE WILL RECEIVE PROPER TREATMENT IF SHE STAYS WITH THE MOCKLEYS?

I . . . UH . . .

I COULDN'T THINK OF A BETTER PLACE FOR A HORSE TO REACH ITS FULL POTENTIAL THAN RIGHT HERE AT SUPERRIDE.
MR. MOCKLEY HAS PLACED THE RESPONSIBILITY OF THESE HORSES IN DINO'S AND MY HANDS. ISN'T THAT RIGHT, MR MOCKLEY?
UH . . . YES, OF COURSE . . . THAT'S RIGHT. I'VE NEVER SEEN MORE CAPABLE HANDS . . . UH, STABLE HANDS.
AND MR. MOCKLEY HAS MADE PLANS TO EXPAND THE STABLES AND PADDOCKS SO THAT ALL THE HORSES HAVE ROOM TO GROW.
HE HAS?
I HAVE?
IF THIS IS TRUE, MR. MOCKLEY, THEN YOUR GENEROSITY WILL NOT GO UNNOTICED AT NEXT YEAR'S HEWITT HORSE SHOW.
WELL . . . UM . . . YES, IT'S ALL TRUE. THAT GIRL, MANDY NEVER LIES!

IN FACT, AS SOON AS THE CONSTRUCTION WORKERS ARE DONE WITH THAT RIDE, THEY HAVE ORDERS TO GET STARTED ON THE STABLES.
WE'LL BE BACK TO CHECK ON PROGRESS.

I'M PROUD OF YOU, MANDY.
YOU WERE GREAT. BUT WHY'D YOU COVER FOR MOCKLEY?

SIMPLE . . . THIS WAY I KNOW MR. MOCKLEY WILL LET US KEEP SUNRISE.
AND THAT KEEPS US ALL HAPPY.

LATER, THE REPORTER INTERVIEWS MANDY SOME MORE, AND THIS MAKES SOMEONE ELSE VERY HAPPY.

THE LOCKET! SO THAT'S WHERE IT IS. AND I BET MIRELA AND HER CRYSTAL BALL AREN'T TOO FAR OFF.
4

I'LL BE REWARDED HANDSOMELY FOR THIS.

THE NEXT DAY MANDY IS HAVING SOME FUN WITH FRIENDS AT A NATURAL POOL IN THE WOODS CLOSE TO SUPERRIDE.
WOW, DINO. THAT'S BEAUTIFUL. YOU MUST BE PUTTING IN A LOT OF PRACTICE.
YEAH, THANKS.
HERE COMES A BOMB!
HA HA!
SPLOOSH
GREAT JUMP, LING. I BET MANDY COULDN'T MAKE THAT.
PENELOPE'S TRYING TO GET UNDER YOUR SKIN. JUST IGNORE IT.
NO WAY. I'LL ACCEPT HER DARE . . . IF SHE'S WILLING TO DO THE SAME.
IT'S YOUR DARE, PENELOPE. SO YOU'LL HAVE TO JUMP AFTER MANDY.
IF MANDY HAS THE GUTS TO ACTUALLY JUMP.
YOU CAN STILL RUN HOME TO DADDY, MANDY!
I DON'T THINK SO, PENELOPE.

I HOPE YOU'VE BEEN PRACTICING YOUR BREAST STROKE, PENELOPE. THE CURRENT'S PRETTY STRONG.
THAT WAS FANTASTIC, MANDY!
GRR. . . WE DON'T HAVE TIME FOR THIS!
SORRY, PENELOPE. OF COURSE, IT'S YOUR TURN TO JUMP.
NO! I MEAN . . . IT'S GETTING LATE. THERE'S WORK TO DO.
DADDY WOULD BE VERY UPSET TO SEE YOU ALL SLACKING LIKE THIS.
HEH-HEH. I THINK SOMEONE'S TRYING TO GET OUT OF A DARE.

BACK AT WORK . . .
THANKS FOR HELPING ME, MANDY. AFTER ALL, IT IS PRETTY LATE.
I GUESS PENELOPE WAS RIGHT. WE DID SPEND TOO MUCH TIME AT THE CREEK.
AT LEAST WE HAD FUN. IT WAS DEFINITELY WORTH IT.
YEAH, I THINK SO TOOOOOOO!
DINO! ARE YOU OK-
CRRRRRRAAACK
RRRUMBLE
OOF!

ARE YOU ALRIGHT?
YEAH. THANKS FOR BREAKING MY FALL.
A TUNNEL UNDER SUPERRIDE?
LOOKS OLD, TOO.
MANDY, WHERE ARE YOU GOING?
EXPLORING! COME ON. LET'S SEE WHERE THIS LEADS.
OH NO. THIS MEANS THERE'S DANGER UP AHEAD.
BZZZZZ
WHO'S THERE?
HMMM . . . TWO BUSYBODIES. LET ME TELL YOU KIDS SOMETHING. THERE'S MAGIC IN OLD THEME PARKS . . .

. . . AND GHASTLY THINGS HAPPEN TO BUSYBODIES WHO GET IN THE WAY.
QUICK, MANDY. TURN BACK! WE NEED TO GET OUT OF HERE.
COME ON, MANDY. WE NEED TO TELL MIKE ABOUT THIS!
DON'T TELL MY DAD I WAS WITH YOU. HE'LL GET UPSET IF HE THINKS I WAS IN DANGER.
OKAY, I PROMISE. BUT WHERE ARE YOU GOING?
UM . . . *COUGH COUGH* - I JUST NEED SOME FRESH AIR. SEE YOU TOMORROW.
DINO TAKES MIKE BACK TO THE SPOT WHERE THE HOLE WAS.
THAT'S ODD. IT WAS RIGHT HERE!
SURE, DINO. I BELIEVE YOU.
?
WHERE'D IT GO?
POOR KID. MOCKLEY WORKS HIM SO HARD HE'S STARTING TO IMAGINE THINGS.

NOT TOO FAR AWAY...
THE COAST IS CLEAR, MIDNIGHT. NOW'S OUR CHANCE TO INVESTIGATE.
WE'LL JUST HAVE TO BREAK IT OPEN AGAIN.
NOW LET'S GET TO THE BOTTOM OF THIS.
OH NO, MIDNIGHT. YOU CAN'T FIT THROUGH.
NEIGHHH!

NEEEIGHHH!
OH, REALLY? YOU'LL BE ABLE TO FOLLOW ME ABOVE GROUND AS I GO ALONG THE TUNNEL?
OKAY THEN, MIDNIGHT. BE CAREFUL, AND GOOD LUCK!
THIS ABILITY TO UNDERSTAND HORSES IS SO AMAZING.
I'M ALMOST AT THE POINT WHERE I SAW THAT STRANGE MAN.
THE TUNNEL SPLITS. COULD THIS BE WHAT HE WAS HIDING FROM US?

LET'S SEE WHERE THIS LEADS . . .
GASP! THIS IS MY BEDROOM!
A TRAP DOOR? BUT . . . WHAT COULD HE BE LOOKING FOR IN MY ROOM?
WHATEVER IT IS, HE'S NOT GOING TO GET IT THAT EASILY!
SQUEAK
MIDNIGHT, HE WAS IN MY ROOM! WHAT DO YOU SUPPOSE HE WANTED?

WHAT ARE YOU UP TO IN HERE, MANDY?

NOTHING, DAD. I JUST THOUGHT I'D. . . REDECORATE.

REDECORATING, EH?
I NEED A CHANGE.

I COULD HELP.
DON'T BOTHER. I LIKE IT THE WAY IT IS NOW.
YOU CAN BE REALLY FICKLE AT TIMES, MANDY.
MANDY
I'M JUST AT THAT AGE, DADDY. HA HA! GOOD NIGHT.
KIDS THESE DAYS SURE ARE STRANGE.
PHEW! THAT WAS A CLOSE ONE. COME ON, MIDNIGHT. . .

LET'S FIND OUT WHERE THAT OTHER TUNNEL LEADS TO. YOU FOLLOW UP ABOVE.
THIS ROOM LOOKS FAMILIAR TOO.
THIS IS MADAME ZINGARA'S HOUSE!
SCRRTCH SCRRRTCH
WHAT'S THAT SOUND?
SCRRTCH SCRRTCH
MADAME ZINGARA? IS THAT YOU?
GASP
KITTY! YOU NEARLY GAVE ME A HEART ATTACK!

I WONDER WHY MADAME ZINGARA KEEPS PICTURES OF MY MOTHER WITH HER CRYSTAL BALL . . .
I'LL TAKE THAT. THANK YOU, YOUNG LADY.
MIDNIGHT! HELP!
CRAASH
AAAAARRGH!

NOW, WHO'LL STOP ME?
OOMPH!
UNCLE MILOSH?
NOBODY CAN STOP ME NOW!
POOFF
<COUGH COUGH>.
MADAME ZINGARA! MIDNIGHT AND I TRIED TO STOP HIM . . .
BUT HE STOLE YOUR CRYSTAL BALL!
THEN WE MUST GET IT BACK.

FUN 'N GAM
REFRESHMENTS
WHO IS THAT MAN, MADAME ZINGARA?
HE IS MY UNCLE, MILOSH.
HE WANTS THE CRYSTAL BALL BECAUSE IT'S CONNECTED TO THE MAGIC, ISN'T IT?
AND HE WANTS TO DESTROY THAT BOND WITH MIDNIGHT.
NOT WHILE I'M HERE!

THERE HE IS!
STAY BACK, MIRELA! OR I'LL DROP THE CRYSTAL BALL OFF THE CLIFF!
YOU WOULDN'T DO THAT, UNCLE MILOSH. YOU NEED ITS POWER.
IF I CAN'T HAVE THE CRYSTAL BALL, NO ONE CAN!
WHAT ARE YOU DOING?

IT'S BURNING MY HANDS!
OUCH! OUCH!
<GASP>.
OH, NO!

BUT . . . IT DOESN'T FEEL HOT AT ALL.
THAT'S BECAUSE THE MAGIC IS WITHIN YOU, CHILD.
NOT FOR LONG!
NEEEEIGHH!
NO! I CAN'T SWIM!

SPLASHHH!

WE MUST GET DOWN THERE, QUICKLY.

LET'S GO, MIDNIGHT.

THE TRAIL ENDS HERE. BUT WHERE IS HE?
HE IS GONE, FOR NOW.
WILL HE BE BACK?
NOT IF HE KNOWS WHAT'S GOOD FOR HIM.
LET'S GO HOME.

BACK AT MADAME ZINGARA'S HOUSE . . .
THANK YOU FOR HELPING ME, MANDY.
THAT'S OK.
WHAT IS THIS, MADAME ZINGARA?
IT'S THE SYMBOL . . .
. . . OF THOSE WHO HAVE PROMISED TO PROTECT THE MAGIC.
THOUGH UNCLE MILOSH HAS CHOSEN TO WALK THE PATH OF DARKNESS, REST ASSURED THAT I WILL PROTECT YOU.
AS SO MANY ZINGARAS DID BEFORE ME, I WILL MAKE SURE THE MAGIC IS SAFE WITH YOU.

THAT BRAT SPOILED EVERYTHING. BUT AS LONG AS THE MASTER DOESN'T FIND OUT THAT I -
FIND OUT WHAT, MILOSH?
MASTER?!?
I AM SORRY, MASTER. I KNOW I WAS ONLY MEANT TO OBSERVE THE TARGET, BUT -
BUT YOU GOT OVERCONFIDENT.
I SHOULD HAVE WAITED. I SEE THAT NOW, MASTER.
NO MATTER. YOUR NIECE MAY KNOW YOUR INTENTIONS, NOW . . .
. . . BUT NOT EVEN HER CRYSTAL BALL CAN PREPARE HER FOR WHAT I HAVE PLANNED. MWAH HAH HAH!
END!

Carousel